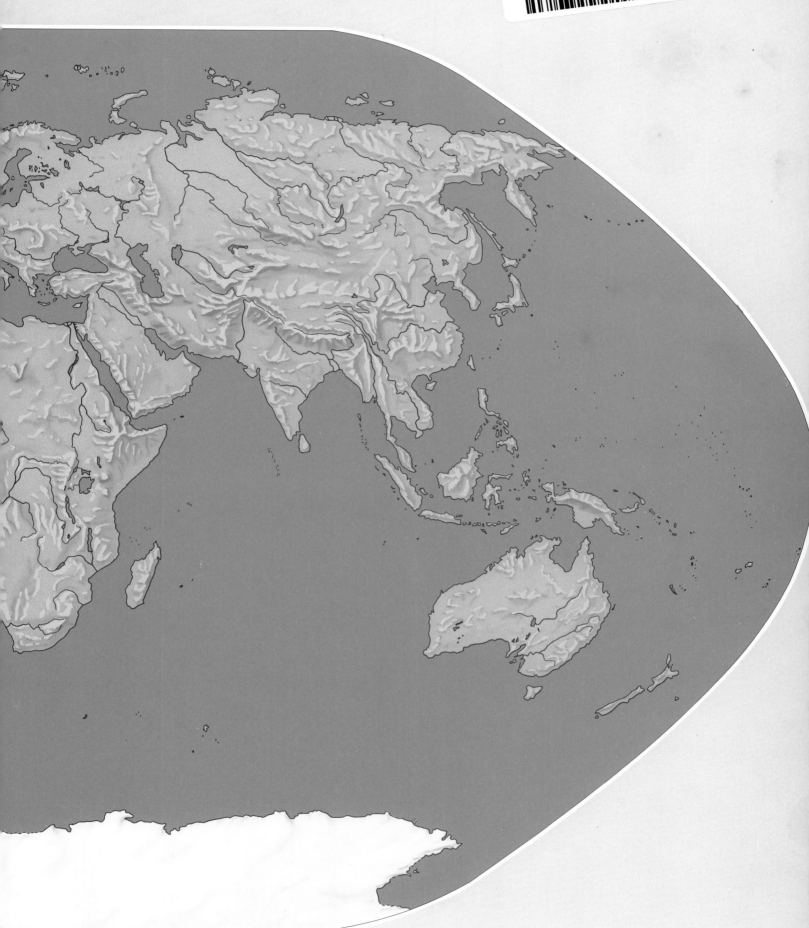

My Story Book of Long Ago

First Published in 1983
© Text R J Unstead 1983
© Illustrations Ivan Lapper 1983
ISBN 0 00 195383 4
Printed in Italy by New Interlitho

William Collins Sons & Co Ltd
London · Glasgow · Sydney · Auckland
Toronto · Johannesburg

My Story Book of Long Ago

R. J. UNSTEAD

Illustrated by
IVAN LAPPER

COLLINS

This book is about Tom and his grandpa. In it you will find the stories that Grandpa told Tom about a long time ago.

There are stories about what life was like during the last War and what it was like when Grandpa was a boy. And there are stories about how people lived even before that.

Some of the stories are about things that Grandpa remembered, but others are about what he'd been told or what he'd read. But all the stories in this book are about the past.

One day in the holidays, Tom went round to his grandparents' house, where he met Grandpa coming out of the front gate with the dog.

"Hello, Grandpa," said Tom. "Can I come with you?"

"Of course you can, Tom," replied Grandpa, "We're just going up to the park for Nip's morning run. Here, you can take his lead."

They went down the road and turned left into Gun Lane, leading to the park.

"Why is it called Gun Lane?" asked Tom.

"Because there was an ack-ack gun up in the park during the last War."

"Grandpa, please will you tell me about the War?"

"Now, let me think," said Grandpa. "When the War started in 1939, we were living here in London. I had left school and had started work in the printing trade."

"The first thing I remember about the War was seeing hundreds of children lined up waiting to be evacuated — that is, to be taken by bus and train to some place in the country where they would be safe from bombs.

Every boy and girl had a label tied on their coat with their name and address in case they got lost. Each one had a little suitcase or a paper parcel of clothes and a cardboard box with their gasmask in it.

Everyone was supposed to practise wearing their gasmask and there were special ones for babies — and even for dogs and cats. When the buses moved off, the mothers and grandmas cried.

At the top of our road there was that ack-ack gun I told you about in the park. We had an air raid shelter in the garden and when the sirens went to warn everyone that the bombers were coming over, we used to take rugs and blankets (and Timmy, the dog) and go and sit there. Here you can see some people spending the night sleeping in an Underground Tube station because it was safer down there than in their houses."

"Up in the sky, there were barrage balloons. Important buildings had sandbags round them, and big windows had to be crisscrossed with sticky tape to stop broken glass flying about.

At night, the streets were almost pitch-dark, because the street lamps were not allowed to be on, because they would give away the position of towns to the enemy. This was called the Blackout. Air Raid Wardens knocked at the door if there was a chink of light from one of your windows. We often saw searchlights trying to find an enemy bomber.

In the morning after an air raid, we sometimes saw houses in ruins or still on fire. Once, we saw a London bus upside down. Everyone had to have a ration book, showing how much meat, sugar, butter, eggs and so on they could buy in the shops. The baby had a green book; children had blue ones. Even sweets were rationed. You had one bar of chocolate a week if you were lucky. Children helped in lots of ways during the War. Scouts filled sandbags and ran messages. Girl Guides used to roll bandages and knit socks for the troops.

In the summer holidays, some children went to Harvest Camps to help the farmers. Others went round collecting things made of metal, as well as rags, wastepaper, bottles and so on. Instead of being thrown away, rags and wastepaper were turned into clean new paper; bottles were used again; aluminium saucepans helped to make an aeroplane and people's garden railings were melted down to make tanks.

One day, a letter came telling me I had been called-up for the Army. I was rather glad, really, and, after a lot of training, I passed out as a driver. I was posted to Italy, where I learned to drive an armoured car.''

''Did you get wounded in the War, Grandpa?'' asked Tom.

''No, I was lucky. Once, as we were entering a little town near Naples, we were hit by a mortar shell. My mate, Ted Miller, lost his left arm, but the rest of us escaped with a few cuts and bruises and we all got home safe and sound.

When the War ended, we had a party in our street. People put tables down the middle of the road. Children wore fancy dress and all the houses were decorated. After dark, there were fireworks in the park.''

Next day, as Tom and Grandpa went for their walk together, Tom said, "I liked hearing about the War. Please tell me about when you were a boy about as old as me."

"Now, as far as I can remember," said Grandpa, "it would have been in 1927 when we lived at Number 58, High Street, Barnstock, where my dad had a grocer's shop.

Dad worked in the shop, with two assistants — Mr Bean and Miss Watson. There was also Sidney, the errand boy, who took groceries to people's houses. He rode a bicycle with a basket at the front and he used to whistle all the time. Mum didn't often help in the shop, because she was always busy in the kitchen. On washdays, she used to let me turn the mangle.

This is a picture of the inside of our shop. Dad is slicing bacon on the bacon-slicer and that's Miss Watson putting butter on the scales. All the tradesmen — the butcher, the milkman, the coal merchant, the baker, the greengrocer — came round with a horse and cart. Mr Marsh, the milkman, filled your jug from the milk can and, sometimes, he let me have a ride on the cart."

Tom's grandpa went on . . .

"I remember our first wireless set. It had a horn or you could listen with headphones on. We didn't have electric light in our house or in the shop, but gas-lamps, which made a soft hissing sound.

Mum let us go to the pictures sometimes (it cost 1p) to see Charlie Chaplin. But, on Sundays, we all had to go to church in our best clothes – that's when Dad wore his bowler hat. I remember school. You had to sit still, and pay attention. Boys got the cane for talking.

Sometimes, someone would shout, 'Look, an aeroplane!' We'd all stare up into the sky and give a cheer when it came over. Once, I saw a seaplane.

There was a lot in the papers about a man called Lindbergh who flew solo across the Atlantic. Later on, there was a young woman, Amy Johnson, who flew to Australia alone. It took her 19 days.

We never had a car when I was a boy, but my friend Donald's dad had a bull-nosed Morris and they used to take me for a ride. Once, our gran took Daisy and me up to London for the day by train. When we got there, we went to the Museum on a tram.''

"Our gran, or Grandma Amy as we used to call her, had
lived in America when she was a girl and she used to tell us
about her adventures when she crossed America in a covered
wagon, with her parents and her six brothers and sisters.

She gave me this bead belt which she got from an
American Indian. The family started out from a place
called Independence, Missouri, with a wagon train
and took the Oregon Trail to the West. It was a long, very
slow journey because most of the wagons were pulled by
oxen, which didn't walk very fast, and the cows had to be
driven along and milked twice a day. Nearly everybody
walked alongside the wagons, though some of the men
rode horses. People fell ill; oxen died; wagons broke
down and there were always Indians along the trail,
watching. . . .

At night, the Train Captain chose the campsite. Then
the wagons were parked in a circle, their wheels chained
together, so it was safe in the middle for the grown-ups to
light fires and cook supper, while the children played."

"Each wagon was loaded with food for the journey and with all kinds of things people needed for their new homes in the West.

homes in the West.

Indians followed the big wagon train, coming up to ask for gifts of tea, tobacco and sugar. Or they bartered; that was how Amy got the bead belt when an Indian swapped it for a comb.

The Plains Indians lived in villages made up of a circle of tents called tepees. When the buffalo moved to new grazing lands, the Indians moved with them. They strapped the tent poles to the sides of horses, with a sheet of buffalo hide between them to hold their pots, blankets and other possessions. The baby (called a papoose), that you can see in its cradle, travelled on its mother's back.

When, at last, the Pioneers reached Oregon in the West, the first job was to build a home. They had to fell trees, make them smooth on one side and cut notches so they would fit together at the corners.

Logs for the floor were split and smoothed. Windows were a kind of sliding door in the wall but there wasn't any glass. A buffalo hide was fixed over the door to keep the cold out.

Neighbours always came round to help build a house.

It was a hard life, but there was fun when people got together for a wedding or a christening.''

16

The Stone Age

"Grandpa, how do you know what it was like long ago?"

"Well, Tom," said Grandpa, "I know about the last War because I was a young man at the time and I know about the twenties because I was a boy then. Anything further back than that I know because I've been told about it or I've read about it. My Grandma Amy told me about what it was like on the Oregon Trail. It's what grown-ups call history. History is what we know about a long time ago."

"How far back do we know about?" asked Tom.

"Well, the first people we know about were the hunters and food-gatherers of the Stone Age. It was called the Stone Age because the people used stone tools. They collected seeds, berries and fruits to eat and they also killed animals. The hunters, who lived in open-air camps, wore no clothes and had only wooden spears, sharp flints and stone axes. They followed the animals about, dug pits to trap them and used fire to frighten them and make them rush down steep places. Then one or two might get injured and therefore be easy to overtake and kill.

When the weather grew cold, some Stone Age people found caves to live in. They kept the fire alight always, and they wore skins to keep themselves warm.

Mammoth hunters of Russia lived in tents made of animal skins supported by poles and held down by stones and mammoth bones. They carved ivory and bone to make ornaments, beads and needles.

At certain times, they put on masks with the antlers of a deer, head of a bear or skin of a bison and performed dances. They may have done so to please the spirits of the animals or to bring themselves good luck when hunting. Artists painted pictures on rocks and in caves.''

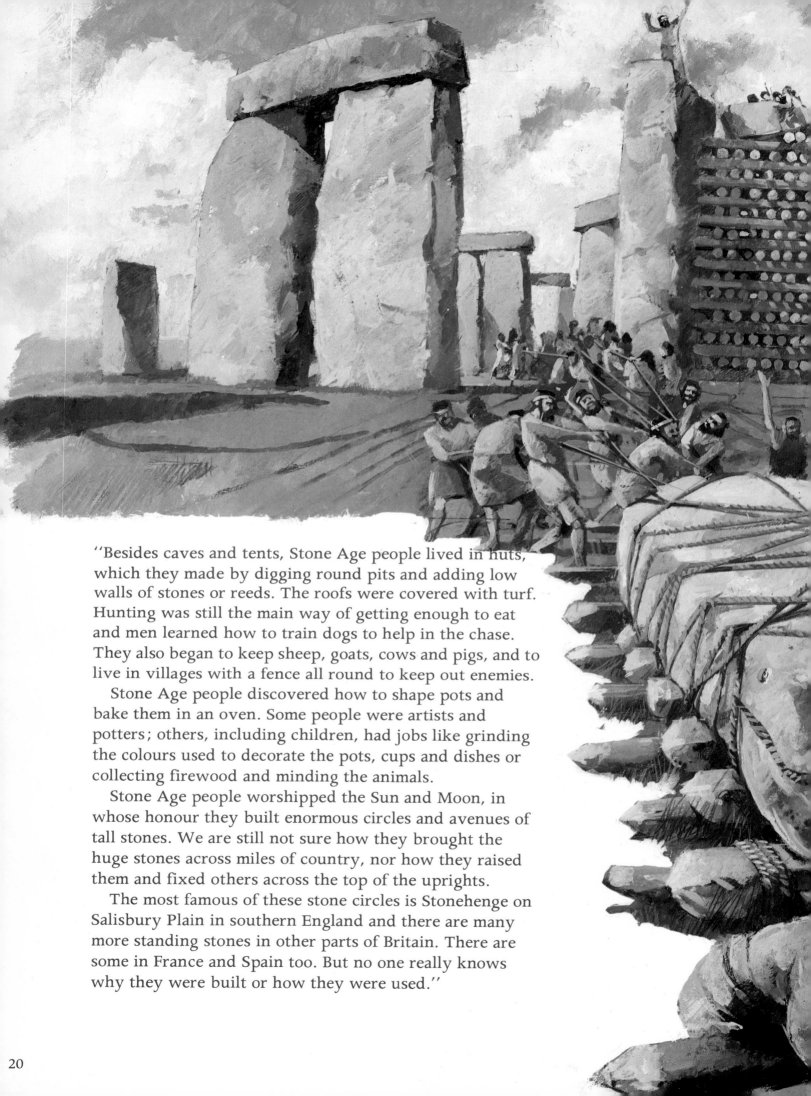

"Besides caves and tents, Stone Age people lived in huts, which they made by digging round pits and adding low walls of stones or reeds. The roofs were covered with turf. Hunting was still the main way of getting enough to eat and men learned how to train dogs to help in the chase. They also began to keep sheep, goats, cows and pigs, and to live in villages with a fence all round to keep out enemies.

Stone Age people discovered how to shape pots and bake them in an oven. Some people were artists and potters; others, including children, had jobs like grinding the colours used to decorate the pots, cups and dishes or collecting firewood and minding the animals.

Stone Age people worshipped the Sun and Moon, in whose honour they built enormous circles and avenues of tall stones. We are still not sure how they brought the huge stones across miles of country, nor how they raised them and fixed others across the top of the uprights.

The most famous of these stone circles is Stonehenge on Salisbury Plain in southern England and there are many more standing stones in other parts of Britain. There are some in France and Spain too. But no one really knows why they were built or how they were used."

Ancient Egypt

"After a long time river valley people in some parts of the world began to live in a different way from the Stone Age people. Instead of always moving about, hunting wild animals and minding a few sheep and goats, they stayed in one place beside their river. They found out how to grow wheat, barley, fruit and vegetables. The soil was good, so there was plenty to eat, and there were fish in the river and wild birds and animals in the marshes. Villages grew into towns and towns into cities.

In Egypt, the River Nile flooded the land every year for about three months. The villages were like islands standing out of the water. Everyone went about in boats made of reeds. When the Nile went back between its banks, it left a layer of rich mud in the fields, in which crops grew very quickly.

This was a busy time for the farmers. They had to plough the land, sow the seed and, later on, harvest the ripe corn.

Everything in Egypt belonged to the King – the land, the building-stone, the gold, silver and all the other riches. He lived in great splendour, for the people looked on him as a god, the son of Ra, the sun god. They bowed down before him

and obeyed his orders. Here you see him seated with his Queen, attended by their servants and officials.

When the King died, his body had to be kept safe for ever in a vast stone pyramid. The Pyramids are the biggest buildings in the world. They are so huge and strong that, after thousands of years, they are still standing on the edge of the desert, not far from the Nile.

Later on, everyone in Egypt wanted to have their bodies placed in a tomb, with lots of goods and riches. The body, wrapped in bandages, is called a mummy."

23

"Seti, who is seven, lives in this house, close to the River Nile. His father is one of the King's officials. The house, built of mud bricks dried in the sun, has several courtyards, an outdoor kitchen, stables, cattle pens, servants' rooms and a chariot-store. Its walled gardens have many shady trees, a summerhouse and a pool with water lilies. The servants, who do all the work, are not paid wages, because the Egyptians do not use money at all. Instead, they are given food, beer, cloth and salt.

Children are treated very kindly in Egypt, so Seti and his sister Shari, who is six, have lots of toys, paintboxes, balls and miniature weapons. Every home has its cats and dogs and, often, one or two pet monkeys.

As a special treat, Seti and Shari go with their father on a fishing trip in the marshes. They move about through the tall reeds, spearing fish and netting wild fowl or bringing them down with a throwing-stick for the hunting-cat to carry back to the boat.

Egyptians love giving parties for their friends, who are served with marvellous roast meats, fish, cakes, fruit, wines and specially brewed beer. Seti, Shari and all the rest of the family are there, even the youngest children, who run about with no clothes on. Hired musicians, singers and dancers entertain the company, but rich Egyptians never join in the dancing; they only watch.

On arrival, the guests are given flowers and cones of sweet-smelling oil they put on their heads. During the party, the cones melt, drenching the guests' hair, face and neck with perfume.''

Ancient Greece

"Not very far from Egypt lived the Ancient Greeks, who were clever people, especially at making pottery and statues, building temples and writing plays to be acted in their open-air theatres. But they were also very quarrelsome. Wars were always going on between different cities. Yet every four years, they stopped fighting, so they could hold the Olympic Games. Then Greeks came from all over the country to take part in horse- and chariot-racing and athletic contests in running, jumping, wrestling, throwing the discus and the javelin. Each winner was given a laurel wreath as a prize."

"In a country, just north of Greece, lived a people called the Macedonians. Here you can see their King's palace yard, where a magnificent horse called Bucephalus plunged and reared as half a dozen grooms tried to control him. Not one of them could stay on his back. Suddenly, a boy, aged about twelve, ran from the crowd of onlookers and seized the rope from a startled groom. 'Let me have him,' cried the boy, 'I can ride him!'

He led the King's new horse away from the noisy crowd, stroking his neck and talking to him softly. Then the boy turned the horse's head so it could no longer see its own shadow. That had been why it was terrified. Once under control, the horse let the boy leap on its back and ride to where the King stood watching.

'He is yours!' shouted the King to the boy who was his son. 'One day you will ride him to conquer kingdoms!'

The boy was Alexander and he became king at the age of twenty, when his father died. He took control of his father's army which had beaten the Greeks. The Greeks did not see why they should obey a leader so young, but Alexander swiftly punished those who dared to disobey him.

Then Alexander collected an army of Greeks and Macedonians and marched away to attack the Persians, who lived in a country nearby. Mounted on Bucephalus, he defeated their huge armies in one battle after another. He went on and on, conquering kingdoms, seizing their treasures, founding new cities and marching east until he reached India. There he won a great victory over the Indian princes and, after Bucephalus had died and been given a magnificent funeral, Alexander turned back.

This brilliant general suddenly caught marsh fever. As he lay dying, his soldiers filed past his bed to salute their general for the last time: Alexander the Great.''

Roman Times

''About 300 years after Alexander the Great's death, Greece and many other countries came to be ruled by the Romans.

Here is Marcus, son of a Roman lawyer, at school. There are only twelve boys in the class, but their teacher is very strict and hits them on the hand with his rod if they make a mistake.

The main lessons are reading and writing. Marcus writes with his stylus (pen) on the wax tablet. It can be smoothed over after his work has been corrected. Arithmetic is done on a bead counting frame called an abacus. The boys have to learn to read and write Greek as well as Latin.

After school, the slave takes Marcus to the Baths, where he and the other boys undress and rub themselves all over with oil. Then they go to the exercise yard to run races, wrestle and learn boxing. When they are hot and sweaty, a slave scrapes off the oil and dirt and they dive into the swimming pool. After that, they go through the cold room, into the warm room and then the hot room. Finally, Marcus takes a cold plunge, before getting dressed. Then he goes home across the Forum, the town square, past the shops, statues and important buildings.

Marcus's father is rich, so his home is in the main street. Its front door, guarded by a slave and a fierce dog, opens into the hall, in which there is a shallow pool and the walls are decorated with patterns in bright colours. Marcus goes through to the garden, where he finds his mother and his sister Julia playing with the younger children on the terrace. He bows politely to his mother and a slave brings him a dish of little cakes, olives and roasted nuts. Julia doesn't go to school like Marcus, but has lessons at home from her mother and from a visiting teacher.

The house is cool in summer because the hall is open to the sky and most of the rooms face on to the hall or the garden. In winter, the main rooms are warmed by central heating. Slaves stoke a furnace from which hot air passes under the floors and up through hollow bricks in the walls.''

"Going about town, Marcus often sees soldiers on leave or doing guard duty at the main gates, for Rome has the best trained army in the world. That is why the Romans have conquered so many countries.

An ordinary soldier belongs to his regiment, or legion, and is therefore called a legionary. He wears a helmet, breastplate, tunic and hobnailed boots and is armed with a curved shield, a short sword and two throwing-spears.

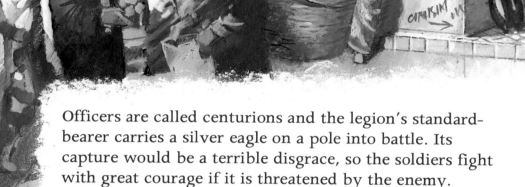

Officers are called centurions and the legion's standard-bearer carries a silver eagle on a pole into battle. Its capture would be a terrible disgrace, so the soldiers fight with great courage if it is threatened by the enemy.

Like most towns in the Roman Empire, Marcus's town has several places where people can go to enjoy themselves. For those who like plays, music and shows with dancers, jugglers and acrobats, there's the theatre, where the audience sits on stone benches arranged in a semicircle.

At the circus, outside the walls, Marcus likes to go to an athletics meeting or, better still, to the chariot races, which are tremendously exciting. Everyone has their favourite charioteer, who is usually a famous hero and very rich.

The Amphitheatre is a huge round building where thousands of people go to watch boxing matches, mock battles and real fights between pairs of gladiators, who are mostly slaves and criminals. Often, a man armed with only a net and a trident, fights another wearing a helmet and leg- and arm-guards and armed with a sword until one is killed.

As a change, wild animals, such as lions, tigers, bears and bulls, are let into the arena to be shot by archers or attacked by dogs. Today we think these bloodthirsty sports are very cruel and they are no longer allowed."

The Vikings

"After the Romans had ruled a great part of the world for a long time, their Empire was destroyed by tribesmen whom they called barbarians. The fiercest people in Europe came from Sweden, Norway and Denmark. They were called Vikings and the boys had names like Ulf, Ragnar, Sigurd, Blue-tooth Harold and Magnus Bare-legs, while girls were called Brynhild, Aud, Gudrid or Halga the Fair.

At home, the Vikings lived in long wooden houses, with roofs made of turf which often went right down to the ground. A house had only one room, where all the family lived, ate and slept. There were no windows and smoke from the fire in the middle of the floor had to find its way out of a hole in the roof. There wasn't much furniture, just wooden benches and a table. Only a chief had a bed and a chair. Everyone else slept on the floor among the reeds and rushes.

The Vikings had to work hard to get enough food because their farms were small and snow covered the land for much of the year. Children didn't go to school, but girls were taught by their mothers how to sew and weave cloth, to make bread, to cook reindeer stew and preserve meat for the winter by drying it over a smoky fire. A boy had to work on the farm and learn how to handle an oar, swing a war-axe and hurl a spear. At twelve, he was considered to be a grown-up man and fit to go raiding with the warriors.

A wedding, the harvest or the return of warriors from a raid would be the excuse for a feast which often lasted for days on end. Everyone ate huge amounts of food and the men drank ale and mead from drinking horns until they fell asleep or rolled on the floor. Jesters made everybody laugh and minstrels sang of the deeds of famous heroes and how they died in battle and went to Valhalla, Viking heaven."

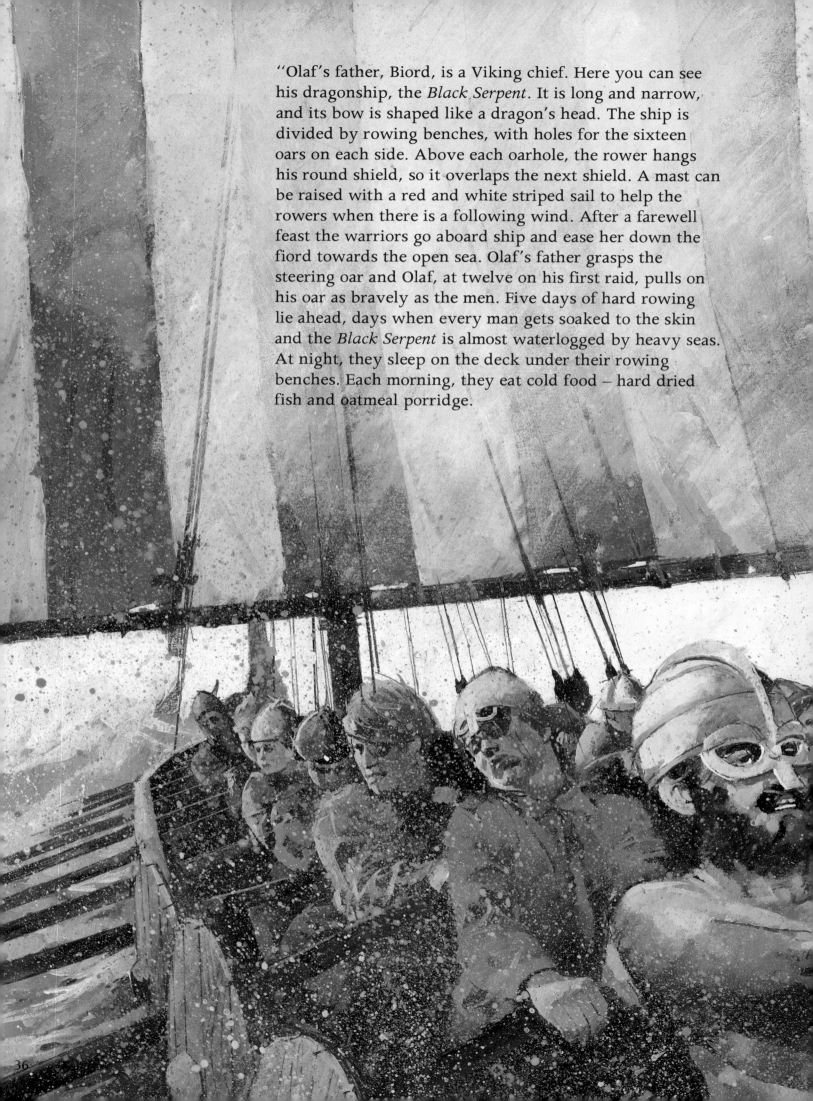

"Olaf's father, Biord, is a Viking chief. Here you can see his dragonship, the *Black Serpent*. It is long and narrow, and its bow is shaped like a dragon's head. The ship is divided by rowing benches, with holes for the sixteen oars on each side. Above each oarhole, the rower hangs his round shield, so it overlaps the next shield. A mast can be raised with a red and white striped sail to help the rowers when there is a following wind. After a farewell feast the warriors go aboard ship and ease her down the fiord towards the open sea. Olaf's father grasps the steering oar and Olaf, at twelve on his first raid, pulls on his oar as bravely as the men. Five days of hard rowing lie ahead, days when every man gets soaked to the skin and the *Black Serpent* is almost waterlogged by heavy seas. At night, they sleep on the deck under their rowing benches. Each morning, they eat cold food — hard dried fish and oatmeal porridge.

After many days they come into a wide bay where a big village stands beside a river mouth. When Biord blows a great blast on his war-horn, the Vikings batter their way into the church where the priest and the people have taken shelter. They take the silver cross, candlesticks and jewelled cups, as other Vikings spread into the village to carry off everything they can. Laden with plunder and driving prisoners before them, the raiders go back to their ships and row out to sea.

At last, they come safely into their own fiord. At home, they boast loud and long of the treasure they have brought back. Olaf's first raid is ended.''

The Normans

"Vikings were also known as Norsemen, a name which was changed to Normans for those who settled in a part of France called Normandy. The Normans were good at building churches and castles and they were hard, tough fighters. The most famous Norman was William the Conqueror, who got his name after he had taken an army across the Channel in the year 1066 and conquered England.

First, he promised a lot of knights that he would reward them if they joined him on this invasion. Then he ordered his men to build a fleet of ships, which were loaded with bows and arrows, swords, suits of mail, horses and the parts of a wooden castle.

The fleet sailed to England, where the Normans landed on the coast and marched inland. No one stopped them, because Harold, King of England, was away in the north, fighting another invader. When Harold heard the news, he hurried back. He ought to have waited to gather fresh troops, but he felt sure he could beat the Normans. They met at Senlac Hill, near the town of Hastings.

The battle went on all day, until, towards evening, the Norman knights broke the English ranks. Harold was badly wounded and many of his soldiers began to run away. But his bodyguard fought on round their dying king until, one by one, they fell dead beside him. After the battle, William was crowned King of England."

"In the time of the Normans, a lord nearly always lived in a castle. It was his home, built to guard his lands and protect his people against enemies. It had a strong tower standing on a mound, inside a courtyard (the bailey), with a stone wall all round. Outside the wall was a ditch or moat, so a visitor had to cross the drawbridge to the main gate.

In the castle lived the lord, his lady, children, knights, pages, men-at-arms, one or two priests and servants. If an enemy threatened, the peasants who lived in nearby villages would come and take shelter at the castle. Even if an enemy got into the bailey, they still had to capture the tower.

The most important room in the castle was the Great Hall. It was rather dim and smoky, because the windows were narrow and the fire was usually made in the middle of the floor. In this picture, you can see the castle household at dinner, served at about 11 o'clock in the morning. The lord and lady sit at the top table on the only chairs in the castle. Everyone else sits on a bench or a stool. The food being brought in has been cooked in a kitchen down in the bailey. Notice the pages waiting at table. They belong to another noble family and have been sent here to learn manners and how to ride and fight.

In the villages round about the castle, all the work on the land was done by peasants or serfs. They were not free to change their jobs, move away or even marry without the lord's permission. They had to work several days a week on his land and, from time to time, give him some money and eggs and chickens. In return, the lord let them have strips of land to grow food on. He also gave them protection against enemies and made sure that everybody obeyed the laws.''

Marco Polo

"In the Middle Ages people knew very little about the outside world and few Europeans had even heard of faraway countries like China.

One day, three tired travellers knocked at the door of a great house in Venice. When it was opened, they said,

'We have come home at last!'

Their own family did not recognize them at first, because they had been away for 24 years. Their names were Nicolo, Maffeo and Marco Polo and they had travelled all the way from China.

When they had set out, Marco was seventeen years old and making his first journey with his father and his uncle. There were so many delays and dangers from storms, deserts, wars and robbers that it took them three and a half years to reach China! Here you can see them crossing the Gobi desert, with some other merchants and hired guards. Travellers greatly feared this desert because it was so vast and lonely that it was easy to get lost. Donkeys were better than horses on such a hard journey and the two-humped camels could go long distances without water.

On reaching China, the Polos were taken before Kublai Khan, the Emperor or Great Khan, who greeted them kindly at his Summer Palace at Shang Tu.''

"Kublai Khan took such a liking to young Marco that he gave him the job of travelling all over China as an inspector. Marco found that it was a huge country, with many rivers, canals, seaports and cities, nearly all of them far bigger than any in Europe.

44

Marco found the Chinese people friendly and polite. They were not as fierce and quarrelsome as Europeans. While an Italian or a Frenchman always wore a sword or a dagger, no one in China carried weapons, except soldiers.

Here is Marco Polo on his travels. He saw many gorgeous palaces and temples, great carriages with silken curtains, painted barges, huge four-masted junks, printed books, silkmaking, the Khan's express letter service, fireworks, hand grenades, marvellous paintings, paper money and 'black stones that burned like logs'. The black stones were coal, which he had never seen before.

After they got home and were welcomed by the family, the Polos took a bath and changed into new clothes. Then they sent for their ragged old clothes and, with a knife, slit open the seams. Out poured the jewels and precious stones they had brought back! These were the riches they had earned in the service of the Great Khan.''

The Discovery of America

"After Marco Polo's travels people knew that there was such a place as China and also India and the Spice Islands. They wanted to trade with these distant countries, but the journey was extremely long and dangerous.

An Italian sailor named Christopher Columbus thought that the best way would be to sail *west* across the Atlantic Ocean. This was a completely new idea because in those days not many people believed that the world was round. Also, sailors did not like sailing far out of sight of land. No one took much notice of his idea until King Ferdinand and Queen Isabella of Spain offered him three ships with crews and the necessary stores for the voyage.

In August 1492 Columbus set sail into the Atlantic. As the days and weeks went by, the sailors grew frightened. They feared they would sail over the edge of the world and told Columbus to turn back. He begged them to keep going for just three more days. Next morning, they saw a land bird flying and a branch with green leaves floating by. On October 12th, just before dawn, a lookout shouted, 'Land ho!' There was an island, with a sandy beach which was soon crowded with brown men and women who came running to the water's edge to welcome the strangers.

Columbus was puzzled. He expected to see a great seaport, splendid cities and civilized people. But he landed on the island, put up the Spanish flag and gave presents to the local people. He called them 'Indians' because he felt sure he had reached an outlying island of the Indies, not far from China. They gave him fruits, green parrots and some arrows, but there was no sign of gold. He captured seven of the men and sailed on to another island. But this wasn't China either.

When Columbus got back to Spain, the King rewarded him richly. He made three more voyages but, to the end of his life, he never knew that he had discovered the way, not to China, but to America!"

"At the time of Columbus's voyage, there were living in that part of America called Mexico a people called Aztecs. Short, strong and very hard-working, they had built a marvellous capital on some islands in a lake. It was a city of white buildings, towers, pyramids and temples to the Aztec gods, which had names like Lefthanded Humming Bird and Plumed Serpent. People went about in boats along canals which served as streets. Their name for the city was Place of the Prickly Pear Cactus. The Aztecs were clever goldsmiths, potters and builders. They made beautiful feather cloaks, headdresses and banners which you can see in this picture, using millions of feathers from tropical birds.

Aztec children went to school to learn to sing, dance, study the stars and obey their elders. Girls were taught by their mothers to spin thread by the age of seven. Later they learned to cook, weave and run a house so they were ready for marriage at sixteen.

Boys learned how to use axes, slings and swords and how to fight. Here you can see two boys practising wrestling. Every boy wanted to become an Eagle Knight or a Jaguar Knight and capture enemies in battle, and take them back to the city where they would be killed to honour the gods. Aztecs believed that unless their gods were given blood, they would not be able to make the sun rise every day. That was why the Aztecs were always at war with neighbouring tribes.

When the Spaniards reached Mexico, they captured the Aztec lake-city, destroyed its great buildings, and stole all its treasures and gold. In spite of their devil masks, most of the Aztecs were killed or died from the Europeans' illnesses.''

The Elizabethans

"After that first voyage of Christopher Columbus, many more sea captains crossed the Atlantic, most of them in the service of the King of Spain. He became the world's richest ruler because the adventurers found plenty of silver and gold in the lands they called the New World. The King said that these lands and all their riches belonged to Spain and that no one else could go there, even to trade or to explore. This made people like the French, the Dutch and the English angry – especially the English!

The Queen of England at this time was Elizabeth I and this is how she and her courtiers dressed. They liked bright colours and fine materials, such as velvet, satin and silk, embroidered with silver thread and semi-precious stones. Children were dressed like grown-ups. Elizabethans enjoyed music, dancing, picnics, playing bowls and watching cruel sports like bear-baiting.

Ordinary folk lived in houses built on a framework of oak beams or in little huts of only two rooms, with an earth floor and no proper chimney, only a hole in the roof to let the smoke out. They slept on a straw mattress with a log of wood for a pillow and had little furniture, apart from a couple of stools, a wooden chest and a few pots and pans. Besides the rich, there were lots of poor people in Elizabethan England. Beggars and gangs of robbers roamed the streets and countryside, causing the Queen to pass laws to help the poor and to make farmers grow more corn for food instead of keeping sheep for wool."

"Queen Elizabeth's most famous sea captain was Francis Drake, a fine navigator and a hard ruthless fighter. He robbed the Spaniards at sea and attacked their settlements ashore in America.

In his ship, the *Golden Hind,* Drake sailed down the coast of South America and into the Pacific Ocean, where he attacked the Spanish ships and filled his hold with plunder, before sailing on to the East Indies. Here he exchanged some of the stolen silver for spices.

After three years, he arrived back in England, with so much treasure for the Queen that she knighted him on board his own flagship.

A different kind of hero from Drake was Ralph Fitch, a London merchant who travelled in the opposite direction to India. He managed to reach Fatehpur Sikri, the beautiful red sandstone city of Akbar the Great. Akbar was famous for his skill in riding elephants on tiger hunts and for taking part in contests between fighting elephants. Ralph went to the royal palace, where Akbar, who was not only brave, but wise and merciful, gave audience to important visitors and to poor persons as well. Notice the scribe writing down every word that the great Emperor speaks."

The Pilgrim Fathers

"In the reign of Queen Elizabeth's cousin, King James I, a girl called Priscilla Mullins, her little brother, Joey, and their parents sailed from England in an old ship called the *Mayflower*. Altogether, there were 102 passengers on board – men, women and children, who brought with them provisions, tools, guns, pigs, goats and chickens, because they meant to settle in America.

After a rough voyage that lasted 67 days, the Pilgrims (as they were called) landed at a place named New Plymouth, where there was wooded country with a good stream. There was no sign of Indians, although they found a few empty huts and some half-buried baskets of corn. Winter was coming on, so the first task was to build homes to live in.

The next task was to build the Common House as a Church and a meeting place for all the people. It was made of wooden planks with a thatched roof. After it was finished, they dragged cannons up to the top of a steep hill and built a fort, because they were frightened of attacks by Indians."

"That winter, the weather was bitterly cold and the settlers were soon short of food. Parties went out hunting, but they didn't have much luck and some of the Pilgrims began to fall ill. Priscilla's mother and father were among the first to die and, after them, her dear brother Joey. By the time spring came round, only seven persons were well enough to look after the others. All the wives except four, had died and nearly all the children were orphans.

Priscilla made her home with William and Mary Brewster. One morning, when she was out in the woods picking wild berries, she heard a sound behind her. Turning she saw an Indian, armed with a bow and arrows. To her astonishment, he smiled broadly and said,
    'Me Samoset'
    The Indian had learned English from sailors along the coast and, next day, he came back with another Indian called Squanto. He showed the Pilgrims how to plant Indian corn, how to set traps for deer, the best places to catch fish, which berries and fruits were safe to eat and how to make a drink from a plant called sassafras.

At the end of the first summer, the Pilgrims had a
Thanksgiving feast. The men shot plenty of wild turkeys,
ducks and geese. The women baked cornbread and cooked
eels, shellfish, wild plums and cranberries which the
children gathered in the woods. They invited their friend
Squanto and the Chief of a local tribe who brought along
90 braves, carrying five deer for the feast.

Afterwards, the Pilgrims sang hymns and
songs. Then the Indians gave a display of dancing. At the
end, the Pilgrims' Captain fired the cannons on the hill,
much to the astonishment of the Indians, who were
frightened by the noise.

As time went by, more people
came out from England to build their
own homes and start farming.
Priscilla married John Alden, the
carpenter, and they moved to their
own farm at Eagle Tree Pond, where
they brought up their eleven
children.''

1815

"Many English people went to America to start a new life, but for those who stayed behind there were plenty of excitements.

One summer's day in 1815 the Reverend Septimus Fox takes his nephew Ben down to Brighton by stagecoach. They reach Brighton at 3 o'clock and see a lot of people walking along the parade. Down by the beach, there are donkey rides and you can see a few people bathing. They get undressed in huts on wheels and go down the steps into the sea. A drink of sea water is supposed to be good for you!

Along the seafront, Ben sees one of the new bicycles called a dandy-horse. On the green, there is a trotting match and games of shuttlecock and cricket.

Ben's uncle produces a telescope through which they can see some fine ships out at sea – merchantmen from the Indies and warships, like Lord Nelson's *Victory*.''

The Railway Age

"This was the time of many inventions, such as the first steamboats, and the first railway engines like *Puffing Billy,* which pulled coal trucks along a line at a coalmine. Later someone thought of building a railway to carry passengers and goods. They had to have an engine that would go fast and not break down, so they offered FIVE HUNDRED POUNDS for the best steam-engine in some trials to be held on a track at a place called Rainhill.

The winner was the *Rocket,* built by George Stephenson, who is driving his engine in this picture. It reached a speed of nearly 44 mph (70 km). Stephenson and his son Robert went on to build many more engines and to design railways all over the country.

In those days, some people were so poor, they had to send their children to work in factories for a few pence. If the children grew tired, a strapper beat them. If they went

to sleep, they might fall into the machinery. Women and children also worked in coalmines where they had to sit in the dark, opening and shutting doors or they had to crawl along like animals, harnessed to a coaltruck.

Lots of people went out to Australia to look for a better life. They settled in Sydney or across the Blue Mountains in the Outback, where they had to build their own homes like the pioneers in America.''

"In America, about a hundred years ago, a railroad was built across the wild lonely plains and over the great mountain ranges. Now it was possible to travel quickly and comfortably from one side of the country to the other. The days of the covered wagon and the Oregon Trail were over. In this picture we see Amy (Grandpa's Grandma Amy) when she came back to England. She travelled by train to New York and steamship to Liverpool. In her luggage, she had the Indian bead belt which many years later she gave to her grandson."

"Grandpa, could I have another look at the Indian belt?" asked Tom.

"Here you are," said Grandpa, taking it out of the top drawer of his desk, "I've been meaning to give it to you to keep. It will remind you of Grandma Amy and the Oregon Trail and also perhaps of those stories of a long time ago."

Index